C000138276

Project English

Teacher's Book 4

Roderick Hunt & Tricia Kirkham

Contents

© Roderick Hunt and Tricia Kirkham 1990

First published 1990 by Basil Blackwell Ltd, 108 Cowley Road, Oxford OX4 1JF.
Though the whole of this book remains subject to copyright, and may not be reproduced without prior permission of the publisher, permission is granted to photocopy pages 28–38 for use only in the school which has purchased the book.

Blackwell Education

Introduction

Project English has two main aims: to provide opportunities for children to discover for themselves how language works and how they can use it more effectively; and to set English within the context of the wider curriculum.

Project English takes familiar general primary topics and specific language and literature topics as starting points from which a range of English activities are developed. It covers Attainment Targets in the National Curriculum 1, 2, and 3 (Speaking and Listening, Reading, and Writing), and is designed to be used as the basis at Key Stage 2. From it, teachers may build and extend the skills of speaking, listening, reading and writing in line with their own school's policy and the particular needs of their children.

There is an emphasis on open-ended activities which involve group-work and problem-solving. The activities can be adapted to suit a range of abilities; and, at whatever level, they seek to involve the children with their own learning.

The pupil's books

The work contained in the pupil's books covers a wide range of activities based on the six main topic areas. Within each of these six units are three or four linked sections, which develop different aspects of the theme. It is not necessary for children to work, page by page, through the book in order. It is intended that you select work as it is appropriate for your pupils, and as it fits in with other work in the classroom. You may find it useful to use one of the activities as an example or teaching point for a particular language skill, which children can then practise in other work related to their topic or theme. In this way, in line with the philosophy of the National Curriculum, much English work may be done whilst children are working in other subject areas, such as Maths, Science, History, etc.

Information boxes

These can be found throughout the pupil's books. They offer definitions of terms used, or highlight, for the pupil, one of the main learning points of the activity. Sometimes suggestions and encouragement are given to children to transfer this knowledge to other areas of their writing. The aim is to make children aware of the skills and terms they are acquiring and to place them in the wider context of writing, beyond the activity on the page in front of them.

Writers' workshop

This is the last unit in each book. It relates directly to the writing process and deals with procedural and operational aspects, such as the techniques of drafting, writing collaboratively, and approaches to spelling, punctuation and grammar.

Writers' workshop demonstrates to the children ways of looking at writing and provides them with examples that they can relate to their own learning.

The purpose of Writers' workshop is to provide a reference to be used in relation to all the other units. Children and teachers will be able to cross-refer when thinking about particular skills, either as they arise in the course of discussion or as particular points in the information boxes.

The teacher's books

The notes in this book offer information and guidance on the activities in the pupil's book, as well as showing how the work links with the National Curriculum.

Ideas for developing and extending the work are also offered, including activities on photocopiable sheets.

The topic webs give just a few ideas for developing each theme across the curriculum, and are meant as starting points to help teachers wishing to expand their work in this way.

Talking and sharing

Talking, and sharing ideas, is central to the philosophy of *Project English*, and forms the basis of much of the work in each section.

Talking can range from working together with a partner to taking part in a class discussion or debate. It covers group discussion in which children are asked to solve problems, make decisions, express opinions, draw conclusions, advance arguments, formulate questions and work collaboratively on tasks such as writing a story, conducting a survey or making a tape-recording.

Talking should always be to some purpose and it is essential that children regard discussion as a means to an end. Sharing with others is an important aspect of the talking process. It helps children to develop and crystallise their own ideas, and it teaches them to listen to the ideas of others.

If children are unused to talking and sharing, it may be necessary for you to explain carefully what you want them to do. It is probably easier to begin by working in pairs or small groups and children will find it helpful if they know in advance what they are aiming at. It is often a good idea to encourage them to draw up 'points for discussion' so that they work to an agenda or plan.

Some children may also need reassuring that there is not necessarily any one correct answer or outcome; all ideas are acceptable if they can be substantiated.

Discussion groups

Your role, during group discussion, is to monitor what is going on and act as 'enabler'. It may be helpful to join a group if the discussion is not progressing or if you feel it is off the point. In this way you can demonstrate the sort of response you want by asking questions which will help the children to focus more clearly on the issue, or think more carefully about the task in hand.

You might also ask the group to share the main points of their discussion by reporting back, either to the rest of the class or just to you.

The role of the audience (listening)

The role of the audience in discussion may be one children find difficult to assume. It can be helpful to talk to children about listening. Listeners need to sit still and to be quiet and to listen carefully, so that they can make a response at the end. The opportunity to ask questions sometimes gives children an incentive to listen first. When responding to another child's work, suggest that the listeners pick out one or two things they liked, and comment on those. Encourage positive responses and questions: for example, 'What did you mean by...' or, 'Can you tell me more about...'. This kind of question is better than, 'I didn't like...', or, 'I can't understand...'. Good responses are helpful and specific. It may help children understand what you mean if you model some examples yourself. The importance of the role of listener needs to be stressed so that children understand what they have to do and why they are doing it.

Children as writers

Project English provides a wide variety of opportunities for children to become writers but it is not its intention to be prescriptive. Suggestions for particular writing activities are given in the pupil's books, and these all have a purpose in mind. It is hoped, however, that the material will give scope for other writing and that this will arise naturally out of each theme as it develops.

Children, as partners in their own learning, will often take off in new and unexpected directions. Their capacity for thinking widely and creatively is well recognised.

The teacher's role is to enable children to explore and extend every opportunity, and to encourage them to develop each topic. Writing will play an important part in this and, whether children work alone or collectively, teachers should be ready to support and sustain them.

The National Curriculum

There is a chart at the beginning of each unit, which shows some of the Attainment Targets covered by that unit. The charts are intended only as a broad guide for teachers. For Book One, it will be seen that the work covers most of the Attainment Targets for levels two and three; Book Two covers level three; Book Three covers levels three and four, and Book Four covers level four and parts of level five.

Obviously, children may achieve at higher or lower levels than those suggested, and work may be developed or extended to cover other Attainment Targets than those listed.

In the sections on Links with Other Areas of the Curriculum, some of the Attainment Targets for Maths and Science have also been given, where relevant. Again, these are only a broad guide.

Assessment

Photocopiable sheets I, J and K (see pages 36–38) have been designed to involve the children more fully in their own learning. Not only do they provide a record of the work children have done in the areas of speaking and listening, reading, and writing, but they also enable them to review what they have done and to see what areas they might focus on next. In this way children can share in the planning, recording and evaluating of their own work.

The record sheets show the main areas of experience a child will hope to cover in order to achieve a breadth of experience and to meet the requirements of the National Curriculum. They have been specifically designed to allow for flexibility of use and to fit in with new or existing record systems.

Completed sheets could be included in each child's Record of Achievement folder with examples of work clipped to them, and these can be used at parents' meetings to show parents the range of activities their children have covered. You may like to include a system for noting on each sheet areas of particular strengths or weaknesses.

Each sheet contains a space for the children to say what they most enjoyed or what they want to achieve next, plus a very simplified form of review.

The sheets may be used to cover whatever length of time you wish – fortnightly, monthly, half-termly or termly. You may wish to keep them on a regular, well-defined basis, or use them more randomly as a sampling activity.

The children's role in self-assessment

In looking at a record sheet once it has been completed, the child can analyse and discuss areas of work that need attention. Pupil and teacher will be able to see where work has been well covered, and spot any weaknesses together. This can then inform forward planning. Since the child is actively involved in the recording and evaluating process, he or she will more readily see the purpose and aim of future work. In this way the children are involved in negotiating and planning work with the teacher.

Speaking and listening (sheet I)

Different types of speaking and listening are given in the stars that surround the rocket. The children may wish to include other categories in the boxes. Recording is done in the appropriate sections.

Reading (sheet J)

For this, children fill in titles from their most recent reading, with the dates, in the appropriate sections.

Writing (sheet K)

Here a colour-code system could be devised for the processes set out on the satellite, with children colouring in the small boxes on the rocket to indicate what stage of the writing process they have reached.

Thoughts and feelings
(theme: Ourselves)

Pupil's book pages	Activities	Understanding and skills	Attainment targets*
2–3 **Thoughts and feelings**	Discussing extracts	Comparing and contrasting	1.4
		Inferential comprehension	1.5, 1.6
		Style and technique:	2.4, 2.5
	i *The Owl Service*	i Use of dialogue and understatement	3.4, 3.5
		to create fear	3.4, 3.5, 3.6
	ii *The Crane*	ii Description to create tension	4/5.5
	Writing	Personal narrative	
4–5 **Inside my head**	Discussing poems	Empathising	1.4, 1.5, 1.6
		Interpretation	
		Imagery	2.4, 2.5
	Writing:	Personal narrative	3.4, 3.5
	Personal response	Description	
	Story or poem	Ordering thoughts	4/5.5
6–7 **Inside and out**	Discussing poems	Comprehension	1.4, 1.5, 1.6
		Analysis	2.4, 2.5
	Writing: story or poem	Recounting personal experiences	3.4, 3.5
		Describing feelings	4/5.5

* Key to Attainment Targets
1 Speaking and Listening
2 Reading
3 Writing

The number before the point relates to the Attainment Target in the National Curriculum. The number after refers to the level.

Focus and aims of the unit

This unit provides the children with an opportunity to identify and verbalise their innermost feelings, and to recognise that others may share similar thoughts and emotions. It also looks at how writers use words to convey feelings.

The first section looks at two extracts about different kinds of fear: one a fear that comes from an unknown source; the other a more identifiable fear that overcomes a boy who has climbed the gantry of a crane. The teaching point for this section focuses on the differences in style between the two passages.

The next two sections use poems to look at thoughts, dreams, fantasies, and how we mask our feelings. The unit allows children to share and discuss their ideas, but it also provides opportunities for personal and reflective writing.

Pages 2–3 Thoughts and feelings

The two passages illustrate contrasting ways of describing the experience of being frightened. Alan Garner uses dialogue to create an atmosphere of tension without ever being explicit. In the second extract, Joan Tate explicitly describes the physical circumstances of fear.

Introducing the section

All children know the feeling of being frightened. Discuss different kinds (and effects) of fear, but do this with care and sensitivity. Fear is not an emotion to feel ashamed of, but there may possibly be one or two children who suffer from strong feelings of fear, or have phobias. They might be disturbed if, say, the fact that some people are terrified of spiders became the subject of amusement or derision among less sensitive children.

You could talk about i) the sort of things that make people feel afraid and ii) what happens to us when we feel afraid.

Differentiate between: feeling nervous; being scared by a spooky story or a frightening ride at the fair; being afraid of things like horses, heights, water, spiders etc.; being frightened by a shock, such as almost falling from a tree, or being narrowly missed by a car; being afraid about something that becomes a worry, possibly a serious one.

Writing

When children have shared some ideas, and come to see that it is quite normal to feel frightened, they can try the writing activity; they are offered a choice of writing from experience or making up a story.

Children could experiment with the two styles exemplified in the extracts in their own writing. They need not necessarily write complete stories (although some may wish to), but try out short scenes or extracts. They could try doing two pieces of writing, one in each style, using the same subject each time. One possibility might be to take 'A frightening ride at the fair' and write two pieces: one a section of dialogue (between two people sitting next to each other on the ride), and the other a description written in the third person, as observed from the ground. Children could try both pieces themselves, or work in pairs. You could suggest a time limit, say 15 minutes. Those wishing to develop their work further could do so at a later time.

Using the information boxes

Both boxes in this unit draw attention to the style of the passages, the techniques used by the authors and the effects they achieve. You could develop the ideas through discussion, and suggest that children look for other examples in reading and library books. These can also be discussed.

The box on page 2, dealing with the use of dialogue, could be linked to the section in Pupil's Book 3 (pages 46–47) which deals with paragraphing speech. Read the extract aloud for children to hear the effect of the broken sentences.

The box on page 3 highlights the differences between the two extracts. In the second extract it is important that every detail is included, to build up a complete picture for the reader. In the first passage the tension was emphasised as much by what was *not* said as by what was said, but in the second piece we know exactly how Nick felt, and can share his fear, because the scene has been so carefully and minutely described.

Extension work

1 Role-play   Some of the dialogues could be used for role-play activities, or conversely role-play could be used first, as a rehearsal for writing.

2 Redrafting   The children's story fragments could be used as an exercise in redrafting. If children have tried one style, suggest, on a different occasion, that they redraft their work in a different style. The pieces of writing do not necessarily have to be published, or polished in any way, as this is an activity to encourage children to experiment and play around with words and style. An alternative is to try redrafting their partner's writing using a different style (with no implied criticism). The strength and merits of each style could be discussed afterwards (in a positive way!).

Pages 4–5   Inside my head

In contrast to the first section, which looked at the outward expression of feelings and emotions, this section looks at the thoughts inside our heads, and at dreams.

You may like to spend some time on the Miroslav Holub poem and go through it slowly with the children, thinking about what it means and considering whether they agree with the poet.

The writing section then asks children about the things inside their own heads. You could begin this activity with a brainstorming session, and then, if you wish, develop it further by asking the children to write a piece of prose or poetry from their brainstorming lists.

Page 5 looks at the unconscious mind, as manifested in dreams. Look at the first poem and discuss the nonsense images and how they are used to express the confusion which often occurs in dreams. The second poem is slightly different; it doesn't use nonsense images, but it is about the impossible, as the second and fourth stanzas state. Ask two children to read the poem aloud, reading alternate stanzas.

Ask: 'How do the second and fourth stanzas qualify the first and third?' and 'What effect does that have?'

This poem could be used in conjunction with page 2, if you wish to focus on the use of dialogue.

The questions move on to dreams. Dreams of this kind can be funny, but equally, they can be disturbing, because of their bizarre nature. The section concludes by asking children to write about a real or made-up dream; this could be written as prose or poetry.

Extension work

1 Working in pairs or groups, the children could continue the Rossetti poem. You might wish to draw attention to the rhyming scheme the poet has used. The work of each group or pair could be put together to make a longer, group poem.

2 You could look at work by Surrealist artists such as Paul Klee or Salvador Dali in conjunction with this section, and suggest that children create their own surreal collages. These could be designed as illustrations to the children's writing.

3 Page 5 could be used for a fuller topic on dreams and nightmares, where the children write more expansively and perhaps compile a class book on the subject. They could also find stories and poems to use as part of this topic.

Using photocopiable sheet A on page 28

The worksheet enables the children to explore nonsense images more fully. It extends the ideas in the poem 'In my dreams', and suggests that children think of some nonsense images of their own.

The ideas here can be extended into drawing and painting. You might like to link it to the creation of ink-blot symmetry (fold a piece of paper across blots of ink or paint of two or more colours), which produces strange and weird shapes. The children can interpret these as nonsense images.

Pages 6–7 Inside and out

The three poems in this section deal with the way inner feelings, powerful as they are, stay bottled up on the inside.

In the first poem, *Silent shout*, some children may well feel a certain sympathy towards the thoughts and feelings expressed. They might be prepared to share their own hidden feelings of reluctance, unwillingness, rebelliousness. Do they think that this is the way the child in the poem always feels, or is it a feeling that is felt occasionally? How is it clear that these are the poet's thoughts and that she is not speaking them aloud? How might the poem be about all children and not just about this one child?

The second poem, *Me*, expresses hidden thoughts; discuss with the children how they know that the poet is doing this and not speaking out loud. Discuss with them the possible situation that prompted these thoughts in the poet. In what way are we to suppose the person is looking at him? Why should one person looking at another provoke a reaction? Why do we feel uncomfortable when we are stared at? Do some people make us feel more uncomfortable than others – if so who, and in what circumstances? Most importantly, ask the children to decide whom they think the poet is really addressing – the other person or himself. How might the poem be an admission of uncertainty or lack of confidence?

The final poem is interesting in that the title, 'The rebel child', is not borne out. The child in the poem affirms the opposite, in fact. Ask the children to discuss this paradox. What is the significance of the third and fifth stanzas? What makes the child in this poem feel a rebel, 'wild as a cloud'? How can the wind and weather affect people's moods? Is it possible to be a rebel if we only feel like one, and don't actually rebel? What form of wild behaviour does the child indulge in? How are the feelings of the poet true of most people?

Writing

The children are given a choice of writing activities, and you should be sensitive to the possibility that some children may find this an opportunity to write something that is intensely personal, and be reluctant to share or publish their work.

With this in mind, suggest that the children might like to follow the steps of rereading their work either with you or with a response partner (see Writers' workshop, Pupil's Book 2). Ask the children to look at style. What style have they used? Why? Does it work? How might it be more effective? Consider making a presentation of the final drafts as part of an anthology in the form of readings, related prose, extracts, music, dance and mime.

Links with other areas of the curriculum

A topic web is not relevant to this section. However, there are a number of areas that might be explored in conjunction with the theme. Possible links are:

dreams
imagination
relationships
emotions
fear
being a rebel
reality and illusions
hopes and ambitions.

Pioneers (theme: Journeys)

Pupil's book pages	Activities	Understanding and skills	Attainment targets*
8–9 **Wagon trains**	Thinking about pioneers and wagon trains	Visualising	1.4
		Making comparisons	1.5
		List making	3.4, 3.5
		Extrapolating	
		Research	2.5
	Conducting an interview	Thinking of questions	1.4
		Using and applying information	1.5
		Role-play	3.4
		Scripting an interview	3.5
		Presenting script	
		Making a recording	4/5.5
10–11 **Hardships and dangers**	Looking at an extract	Problem solving	1.4
		Using evidence	1.5
		Group decision making	
	Looking at a diary extract	Comprehension	
		Interpretation	1.5
		Discussion	2.5
	Imagining hardships (empathising)	Using information	
		List making	3.4, 5.5
		Research	2.4
	Writing a diary	Projecting ideas	3.4
		Personal pronouns	3.5
12–13 **Pioneers' handbook**	Reading a diagram	Writing instructions	2.5
		Problem solving	3.4, 3.5
	Writing a handbook	Brainstorming	
		Group decision making	3.4
		Organising material	3.5
		Summarising	
		Caption writing	4/5.5
		Cross referencing	
		Indexing	

* Key to Attainment Targets
1 Speaking and Listening   The number before the point relates to the Attainment Target in the
2 Reading   National Curriculum. The number after refers to the level.
3 Writing

Focus and aims of the unit

This unit looks at the early pioneers, who made the 2000-mile journey across the continent of North America from Independence, Missouri, to the Pacific Coast between 1841 and 1860. It asks the children to try to visualise the way of life of the settlers and to imagine the hardships, privations and dangers which faced them on their long and hazardous journey.

The unit focuses on making comparisons – between the conveniences and comforts of modern living and the difficulties experienced by those who lived in the days before modern medicine and technology. The aim is to help children develop a 'feel' for a particular time in the past.

A variety of approaches are used, including brainstorming, making lists, planning and role-playing interviews, problem solving, writing a diary, writing a manual or handbook, writing captions and devising instructions.

Pages 8–9 Pioneers

Wagon trains

This section explains who the pioneers were and briefly describes their reasons for seeking a new life and their mode of transport – the covered wagon.

The children are asked to say what they think it would be like to set off on a journey lasting five months, depending on a team of oxen to pull all their possessions across unexplored and rugged country, often in extremes of weather.

Children today will, of course, have little idea of the primitive conditions under which the pioneers lived, and they will have difficulty in conceiving of a slow, lumbering journey of 2000 miles.

Approaching the topic

a) Visualising a long distance.   Ask the children to think of a long journey they have made, the longer the better. Some may have flown to foreign countries for holidays, but a better comparison would be with a car journey. Ask the children to imagine walking such a journey.

Think of a distance of one mile, e.g. from school to the leisure centre. Ask the children to imagine walking that distance, then doing it 2000 times more.

b) Visualising travelling over unexplored country.   Ask the children to imagine visiting a relation but having to walk there by any route other than a road or footpath. What kind of country would this involve crossing? What if they came to a river or stream? How would they cross if there were no bridges?

c) Thinking about the dangers and difficulties.   Ask the children to list what they feel the dangers would have been for the pioneers, e.g.:

Crossing rivers, deserts, mountains and forests.
Having no medical help in case of accident or sickness.
Dangers from wild animals – snake bites, buffalo stampedes, wolves and bears.
Extremes of weather – severe heat and cold, burning sun in the desert, violent storms, heavy rain, snowstorms.
Lack of water when crossing deserts and plains, or lack of fresh water when travelling.
Although there was an abundance of meat and fish, there would have been a lack of other food and provisions.
Having problems of broken wheels and axles, being bogged down in mud or sand or obstructed by rocky terrain.
Being lost and having to retrace their steps.

Each of these can be discussed so that the children begin to appreciate how enormous an undertaking such a journey must have been. Wherever possible, relate the discussion through comparisons to life today. What if your cousins or best friend went on a five-month journey – you would expect a letter or a postcard. Why couldn't the pioneers keep in touch with loved ones at home?

Relating to the problems and making comparisons will bring you to the talking and writing assignment on page 8, where the children are asked to list the modern-day things pioneers would not have had. Here the children could write lists for themselves. Encourage them to put down things in categories – food, communications, medical equipment, transport, etc. Items could include tinned and frozen food, antiseptic cream, wellington boots, drip-dry fabrics, telephones, sliced bread, wrist watches, radios etc.

Talking and writing, page 9

The discussion will prepare the children for the talking and writing assignments on page 9 (devising an interview with a pioneer family that is about to set out). Ask the children to think of some questions. You could role-play an interview. Perhaps you could role-play the part of a pioneer yourself. The children are asked to record or write the interview, so they will need to practise and polish it, possibly writing part or all of it as a script.

Pages 10–11 Hardships and dangers

Stampeding buffalo on the trail

The problem-solving exercise using the passage from *Children of the Oregon Trail* by Rutgers van der Loeff is a 'close-ended' one, in that there is probably only one solution.

The children will enjoy finding the solution more if you spend a little time building up the danger the wagoners are in. Remind the children that the oxen could not move more than a few miles an hour. There was no possibility of running for safety, or out of the path of the stampede. Thousands of buffalo had gathered, and once on the stampede, little would stop them. There had been instances of herds of buffalo plunging over cliffs to their deaths in stampedes. If nothing could be done, the buffalo would charge into the wagons, splintering them like matchwood.

The solution in the story is that the wagoners set fire to the dry grass and the rapid wind-blown fire deflects the buffalo away from the caravan. You might like to read the rest of the chapter to the children if you can obtain a copy of the story.

Amelia Knight's diary, page 11

The diary is interesting in that Amelia Knight records events (such as her son having scarlet fever, the leaving behind of her infant daughter and the death of the last ox) in an almost matter-of-fact way. The questions ask the children to describe their feelings about the journey and to speculate on the kind of family the Knights were.

Talking about dangers and difficulties in more detail could lead to further problem solving, or simply problem analysis. Often we may not have a solution, but nevertheless, analysing problems is a useful and interesting exercise.

Using the information box

The information box points out the difference between first and third person and looks at personal pronouns. In which person is the diary written? Why are diaries written in the first person? There is a unit on Diaries, logs and records in *Project English*, Book 3.

Using photocopiable sheet B on page 29

The children are asked to consider a problem in which they will be expected to role-play pioneers faced with a difficult choice.

There is no clear answer to the problem – any solution being the least of three evils. The children may see that by abandoning two or three wagons and sharing, the pioneers could cross the river in six or eight days, which would get them to the mountains with a week to spare. The children will, in this case, need to discuss ways to cross the river safely and decide the criteria for abandoning certain wagons.

The first thing the children will need to do is to think of particular questions which relate to each alternative. Some they will be able to answer based on fact, some will be answered by opinion.

The children will benefit if they are able to do research, but they will be able to work out a solution simply by using the worksheet. If they use information books (see list at the end of the section) they can find out the answers to questions such as: Was it possible to float the wagons across rivers? How was it possible to haul them over rugged mountains?

Pages 12–13   Pioneers' handbook

How to make a model of a covered wagon

The original instructions are reproduced here for your information.

1   Glue a strong shoebox to a hardboard base that extends 0.5cm all round.
2   Glue balsa strips to box for planking.
3   Drill holes in base to fit wire hoops.
4   Bend wire hoops and push ends into holes.
5   Push spent matchstick pegs into box beside each hoop.
6   Use 1.5cm square wood glued under base for axles, 2 pieces in front, making the lower one 1cm wider.
8   Use 1cm square wood for horse shafts. Cut fabric strips 1 × 3cms, glue to shaft ends leaving tongues to glue between front axle pieces.
9   Make cover 2.5cm longer at each end. Sew in cord and tapes at each hoop. Tie tapes to matchstick pegs. Pull draw cords and tie ends together.

Devising the pioneers' handbook, page 13

To write such a handbook in adult terms would be a very ambitious undertaking. However, if children have access to information books and make use of their problem-solving and list-making sessions, they should be able to produce some interesting work. The project would be a good opportunity to study the geography of the U.S.A. and, in particular, the route taken by the early settlers.

You may prefer to tackle the handbook as a class project, with different groups being responsible for different sections of it.

Books about pioneers and early settlers

Settlers in the American West by Margaret Killingray, B.T. Batsford (Peoples on the Move series).
The American West by Robin May, Macmillan (Colour Library series).
The American West by Richard Tames, B.T. Batsford (Living through History series).
The Prairies by R.R. Sellman, Methuen ('Outlines' series).

An American Pioneer Family by Robin May, Wayland (How they Lived series).
The Pioneers, Time Life Books (The Old West series).
The Splendid Journey by Honore Morrow, Heinemann (fiction).
Children of the Oregon Trail by A. Rutgers van der Loeff, Macmillan and Puffin (fiction).
Onwards to the Oregon by Patricia Yates, Hodder & Stoughton.
Westwards in their Wagons by John L. Foster, Macmillan Education.

Links with other areas of the curriculum

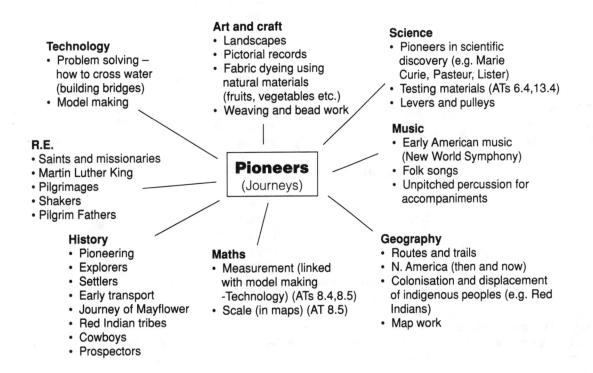

Technology
- Problem solving – how to cross water (building bridges)
- Model making

Art and craft
- Landscapes
- Pictorial records
- Fabric dyeing using natural materials (fruits, vegetables etc.)
- Weaving and bead work

Science
- Pioneers in scientific discovery (e.g. Marie Curie, Pasteur, Lister)
- Testing materials (ATs 6.4,13.4)
- Levers and pulleys

R.E.
- Saints and missionaries
- Martin Luther King
- Pilgrimages
- Shakers
- Pilgrim Fathers

Pioneers (Journeys)

Music
- Early American music (New World Symphony)
- Folk songs
- Unpitched percussion for accompaniments

History
- Pioneering
- Explorers
- Settlers
- Early transport
- Journey of Mayflower
- Red Indian tribes
- Cowboys
- Prospectors

Maths
- Measurement (linked with model making -Technology) (ATs 8.4,8.5)
- Scale (in maps) (AT 8.5)

Geography
- Routes and trails
- N. America (then and now)
- Colonisation and displacement of indigenous peoples (e.g. Red Indians)
- Map work

Hurricane! (theme: Seasons)

Pupil's book pages	Activities	Understanding and skills	Attainment targets*
14–15 **Hurricane!**	Discussing explanation and extract	Comprehension Extrapolating Comparing style and register Use of language: 　nouns 　verbs 　adjectives 　similes	1.4 1.5 2.4, 2.5 3.4 3.5 3.6
	Making a list		
16–17 **All horns and breath**	Comparing poem and explanation	Comparing types of writing Function and purpose Analysing Use of language: 　aptness 　clarity 　order 　imagery 　technical vocabulary	1.4, 2.4 1.5, 2.5 3.4 3.5, 3.6 4/5.5
	Writing		
18–19 **Before and after the hurricane**	Imagining the effects of a hurricane	Projection Visualisation Discussion Decision making	1.4, 2.4 1.5, 2.5
	Planning and recording	Drafting Editing Tape recording	3.4, 3.5 1.4
	Writing an appeal leaflet	Brainstorming List making Planning Style and register	2 3.4, 4/5.5 3.5
	Conducting an interview	Thinking of questions Role-play	1.4 1.5

* Key to Attainment Targets
1 Speaking and Listening
2 Reading
3 Writing

The number before the point relates to the Attainment Target in the National Curriculum. The number after refers to the level.

Focus and aims of the unit

The dramatic and powerful nature of hurricanes offer, as a topic, many opportunities for using and exploring different kinds of writing and language. The unit uses explanations, a diagram, story extracts (which contain part of a radio broadcast) and a poem to examine the functions of writing.

It invites children to look at a topic in depth, to imagine what it would be like to experience a hurricane and to consider its effects on the stricken areas. In doing so it highlights the importance of register and audience, and the value of empathising with a subject.

Pages 14–15 Hurricane!

This section demonstrates three different kinds of register: an explanation, a piece of narrative, and a radio announcement. The questions are designed to provide the children with three things: i) information about the nature of hurricanes; ii) an impression of what the onset of a hurricane is like in terms of its physical power; and iii) what it is like for people who experience the first few frightening hours as the hurricane strikes.

Introducing the topic

Many children will have had personal experience of gales and violent storms. Ask them to give their impression of what it is like to be a) outside in strong wind, and b) in a building during a gale. If you have a book about weather, you will be able to find a chart showing the force of winds at various speeds and the degree of damage at each scale.

You may like to locate Kingston, Jamaica, the Florida coast and other known hurricane areas on a map or suggest that the children look them up in the atlas.

Using the passages

The introduction to hurricanes on page 15 describes the power and destructive force of a hurricane. As such it is a piece of factual writing, conveying information, but even so the writer uses vivid language to create an impression – 'violent', 'danger', 'destroy', 'huge', 'torrents', 'massive', 'bulge', 'like a giant bulldozer'.

The causes of destruction can be summarised simply:

wind
rain } flood
tidal wave

You could talk about this simple summary and ask children to expand and explain it in their own words.

The extract from *Hurricane* by Andrew Salkey gives part of the radio bulletin, and an impression of the power of the wind. Question 5 asks children to list the words and phrases used to describe sounds made by the wind. Remind the children what a simile is. There are three similes used by the writers in this section. Ask the children why similes are used. Can they think of any of their own to describe the force of the wind or the power of the hurricane?

Pages 16–17 All horns and breath

Think about other words for the sounds made by the wind:

howl	shriek	roar
moan	scream	whistle
sigh	screech	breathe.

Ask the children what they notice about these words. Read the poem and link the children's observations to them.

The words in the list above are all sounds made by people or animals and are used of the wind metaphorically. Link the children's observations about them to the theme of the poem by James Berry. Ask the children to comment on the title of this section, 'All horns and breath', and find the line in the poem. Where else in the poem is the hurricane likened to an animal? Is the poet giving us the image of an animal we can recognise, such as a bull, or is he describing something more terrifying with animal-like characteristics? What impression does the poet give us of the animal or monster in the last stanza?

The poem, rich in metaphor and imagery, shares this section with a piece of factual writing – an explanation of the way hurricanes form. This is to allow the children to compare and contrast two very different pieces of writing and to draw conclusions as to their function and purpose.

Ask the children to tell you what kind of writing the prose is. What does the writing set out to do? Explanations have to be very clear, exact and precise. Why is this? How well does this explanation make clear how hurricanes are formed? How important is the diagram? How do diagrams help in factual writing?

Ask the children to compare and contrast the poem and the explanation. How does each one, in a quite different way, tell us about a hurricane?

As a preparation for the writing activity, ask the children to visualise, and then brainstorm the words which describe: how the hurricane spins
the force of the rain
the blackness of the clouds
the calm eye in the centre.

The children might use a thesaurus to help them to expand their lists afterwards.

Extension work

1 The children could plan flow charts based on the explanation on page 17, showing how the hurricane is formed in stages.

2 It can be more difficult to explain a thing than to describe it. Most of us could describe a rain shower, but it is a different matter to explain it, as this requires special knowledge and an understanding of the process involved.

After the children have read the explanation on page 17 more than once, ask them to try and explain in their own words to you or to their partners, how a hurricane is formed.

3 'Translate' the explanation 'How a hurricane is formed' into a poem, using figurative language in the description.

Using photocopiable sheet C on page 30

The questions in the pupil's book concentrate on the differences between the poem and the passage 'How hurricanes form'. Sheet C asks children to look more closely at the passage, make references, and put some of the information into their own words.

Pages 18–19   Before and after the hurricane

Before reading the extract, ask the children to imagine life in the Caribbean, or on the Florida coast. Here the climate is much warmer, so most houses are less substantial. Many are of wooden frame construction, with tin or wooden shingle roofs. People spend much more time out of doors. Ask the children to visualise, then suggest, what might be sensible advice, e.g. nail wooden boards over windows; tie down roofs of large corrugated sheets. Read the extract and compare the instructions with the children's own suggestions.

You will need to explain some of the vocabulary used in the extract, e.g. 'kerosene', 'receptacle', 'batten down', 'divert'.

Using photocopiable sheet D on page 31

The sheet is designed to help children think about the dos and don'ts in the event of a hurricane. The children should write on the sheet in the form of succinct instructions and use arrows or numbers for reference. Children with large handwriting might find it easier to use letters or numbers for reference on the picture and write on a separate sheet. They should still keep their writing as succinct as possible, as if they were writing copy for a printed diagram.

Using the information box

This is an *aide mémoire* about editing. For further details see the Writers' workshop in Pupils' Book 1, and the sections on organising information in the Writers' workshop of Pupil's Book 4, pages 38–41.

Page 19   After the hurricane

The activities ask the children to think about the after-effects of the hurricane. Once again, a brainstorming and visualising session will be helpful in starting the children on these activities. In writing the appeal leaflet it would be helpful if you could obtain some published leaflets (perhaps even hurricane disaster appeal literature) to see what headings and layouts are used, and what kind of language and style.

The role-play activity, if scripted and rehearsed, could form the basis of an assembly, or presentation to parents or other classes.

Extension work

1   Children could write a poem, an entry in a diary, a letter to a friend, or a newspaper report (an opportunity for using desk-top publishing), which describes the after-effects of the hurricane. This will provide an opportunity to write in and compare different styles, formats and registers.

2   The unit as a whole could be extended to include a wide variety of drama activities. It offers scope for factual and imaginative writing, as well as possibilities for tape recording and video recording (such as eye-witness accounts, weather reports, forecasts and so on).

Links with other areas of the curriculum

Art and craft
- Patterns using spray diffusers
- Droplets of paint blown across paper
- Patterns giving sense of movement (geometric and random)

Technology
- Design and make wind sock or weather vane, or windmill
- Devise an emergency communication system

R.E.
- Symbolism of wind (e.g. Pentecost, Holy Spirit) in religious stories and texts

Geography
- Meteorology (hurricane, typhoon etc.)
- Plot areas of recent hurricanes (map work)

Maths
- Probability and statistics (AT 12.5)
- Sequences and number patterns (AT 1.4)

Hurricanes
(Seasons)

History
- Storms at sea, e.g. wrecks, lifeboats
- Grace Darling
- The Armada

P.E. and drama
- Miming movement against wind
- Rescues, dangers and perils
- Movements: gathering momentum and fading away again
- Swirling, twisting, rolling sequences (developing a three-part sequence)

Media education
- Radio broadcasts
- Using cassette and video recorders

Science
- Study of weather
- Climatic regions (ATs 9.4,9.5,12.4)

Outer space (theme: Places)

Pupil's book pages	Activities	Understanding and skills	Attainment targets*
20–21 **Abandoned**	Discussing extract	Inferential comprehension	1.4, 2.4
		Use of vocabulary	1.5, 2.5
	Devising a camera script	Interpreting into another medium	1.4, 1.5, 3.4, 3.5, 4/5.5
	Problem solving:	Group decision making	
	a) Why a boy is abandoned	Giving reasons	1.4

	b) Creating an imaginary
	  planet
		Negotiating and developing
		  ideas
			1.5

22–23 **Strange planets**	Looking at two contrasting passages	Imagining	1.4
		Use of vocabulary	
		Making lists	1.5
		Comparing moods	2.4
		Description	2.5
	Imaginative writing	Writing description	3.4, 3.5, 4/5.5
24–25 **What's out there?**	Discussing poem	Analysing technique	1.4, 1.5
		Interpreting text	2.4, 2.5
	Thinking about space	Personal reactions	
	Writing space poem, story or description	Imaginative writing	3.4, 3.5,
		Asking questions	4/5.5
		Problem solving	

* Key to Attainment Targets
1 Speaking and Listening   The number before the point relates to the Attainment Target in the
2 Reading   National Curriculum. The number after refers to the level.
3 Writing

Focus and aims of the unit

This unit could be a starting point for a science fiction topic on the theme of space and space travel. The aim of the unit is to foster the ability to think creatively and share in the visualisation of imaginative ideas. This provides opportunities for discussion and problem solving, and a variety of writing styles.

In the first section, the children are asked, after reading and analysing a short extract from a space story, to speculate on reasons why a boy is suddenly stranded on a small and lonely planet in outer space. The section broadens into a decision-making exercise which requires the children to decide on the nature of the planet and to put their imaginative ideas into words.

In the second section, the children are asked to compare and contrast two pieces of descriptive writing and to visualise beyond the text.

Jean Kenward's poem 'What's out there?' in the final section leads the children to speculate on the nature of outer space and whether there may be life on planets in other galaxies. The section provides three further ideas for imaginative writing.

Pages 20–21   Outer space

Abandoned

The extract is taken from *Escape from Splatterbang* by Nicholas Fisk.

Children will be able to tackle the group problem-solving exercise on page 20 better if they have some information as a basis for discussion. Questions are provided on photocopiable sheet E on page 32. These will ensure that the children fully understand the extract and have sufficient clues to help them draw conclusions when discussing the possible reasons why Mykl (pronounced Michael) has been left behind.

The questions on page 20 of the Pupil's Book are designed to help children visualise the incident on the planet, and to appreciate the power of the writing.

Children may like to suggest which words and phrases appeal to them and which create the mood and tension of the writing, e.g.:

like the slamming of a great iron door
into harsh ripples and creases
the violet-tinted blackness of the sky.

Discuss with them the use of words such as 'slamming', 'shudder', 'blast', 'harsh', 'thrusting', 'shouted'. What feeling do these words give? Why are they sharp, strong words?

In the second paragraph the children are asked to pick out the words and phrases that describe the starship leaving. These are: 'dwindling', 'shrinking', 'waning', 'receding', 'dying', 'distant', 'pinpoint'.

Again, the children can discuss the effectiveness of the writing, which creates so vividly the impression of the huge and noisy spaceship leaving the planet, and contrast it with the desperation of Mykl left alone on the planet.

The problem-solving exercise on page 20

Why had Mykl been left alone?

Possible reasons will emerge from the group discussion. However, here are some which you may like to use to 'prompt' groups if any are having difficulty.

a) Has Mykl been abandoned for some reason? If so what is it?
   i   As a punishment for a crime on board the starship.
   ii Because he is suffering from some terrible and contagious disease.
   iii Aliens have taken over the starship and killed all the crew except Mykl, whom they have abandoned.
   iv Mykl has been kidnapped by space terrorists and has been put on the planet until the ransom has been paid.
b) Mykl has been left behind by accident for some reason – what might that be?
   i   The starship has landed on the planet to refuel, but has been attacked by aliens. To save the ship, the captain has to give orders to take off. Mykl is unable to get back into the ship in time.
   ii The starship has landed on a strange planet. Mykl, who has been aboard for a long, boring voyage, decides to go out on to the planet for a look round, without informing the captain. To his horror, the ship takes off without him.
   iii Mykl has been left behind simply because the captain has failed to check that the entire crew is safely aboard.

Using the decision-making chart on page 21

Children are asked to decide what they think the planet is like. They will need to negotiate with each other in order to build up a picture of it. Encourage the children to think in detail about the features and dangers and not simply to answer the questions in the affirmative or negative.

Pages 22–23   Strange planets

This section provides opportunities for children to work individually if they so wish, after the two extracts have been read and discussed.

Both passages describe strange planets, but where one appears beautiful, and almost ethereal, the other is bleak and ugly.

Talk about the language used by the author in the first passage. Ask what words the writer uses to convey the appearance of the planet: 'shining bracelet of silvery particles'. 'winked', 'bright', 'like pearls in a necklace', 'blueness', 'brightness', 'flowed', 'beautiful'. Talk about the imagery in the passage – what image is conjured up? (i.e. of jewellery).

A feature of the second extract is that the writer gives a description using negatives. Ask the children to identify each negative. What positive descriptions are there in the passage? What impression do they give of the planet?

The children could think of contrasting names for the planets in the two passages.

The children are asked to write a description of a strange planet for themselves. Insist they write a description only and not a story; if they wish they can extend the description into a space adventure story later.

Extension work

The children may like to have further group problem-solving tasks based on the first two sections of the unit. The extracts from *Escape from Splatterbang* (page 20) and *The Crystal Caves* (page 23) both indicate that survival in outer space is not possible without life-support systems. Mykl is described as wearing an 'echosuit', and Grant lives in a 'space station'.

1 Spacesuits   Ask the groups to think of criteria for the design of a spacesuit. What will it have to be able to withstand? What will it need to be comfortable? What additions would it need as part of its design? How is it more than simply a protective suit? How is it an essential part of the life-support system?

2 Space stations (or survival units) Talk about a survival unit and decide what it would need inside it for a space explorer to survive for a period of time. Decide what items are: a) essential for life (food, water etc.); b) necessary and useful on the planet (tools, radio etc.); and c) useful but not essential.

Pages 24–25 What's out there?

The strength of Jean Kenward's poem 'What's out there?' is the use of a friendly-sounding, slightly jolly rhythm to express some very deep and possibly awe-inspiring thoughts. The poem captures the feelings of wonderment and insignificance that we feel when looking up into space.

Ask children if they have ever stood and looked up into the sky on a clear starlit night. If so, what were their feelings? Were their thoughts similar to those expressed by the poet? Talk about the poem and ask the children to say what they like about it.

The poem is particularly strong in the second stanza. Why might voices call 'softly', when it might seem more sensible for them to shout loudly if they want us to answer them? What is the mood of this verse? In what sense is it about loneliness?

The poem might form the basis of an assembly or an act of worship.

Using the writing ideas of page 25

The ideas suggest three very different types of writing. Ask the children to consider the form their work will take and to think carefully about the effectiveness and power of the words they choose to use. Ask them to remember the five senses. Writers very often describe what can be seen and forget the sounds or smells. Very often it can be effective to write about silence and stillness.

The poems and descriptions could be illustrated and mounted and presented in a space display.

Extension Work

Vocabulary The space theme is an ideal one for thinking about words and their functions.

There are a number of exact technical words which the children can collect and discuss such as: 'galaxy', 'galactic', 'planet', 'interplanetary', 'solar', 'void', 'nimbus', 'stellar', 'interstellar', 'satellite'.

Children can also think of descriptive words about both the beauty of space and the weird nature of some planet they might care to imagine.

Using photocopiable sheet F on page 33 – the space glossary

The glossary contains a number of words similar to the ones suggested above. These words have simple definitions, and the follow-up work asks the children to use some of the definitions given or to write some of their own.

Links with other areas of the curriculum

Art
- Imaginary landscapes (paint and collage, textured weaving)
- Extra-terrestrial beings (clay or Modroc)
- Skyscapes (mobiles using colour wash or wax resist)

R.E.
- Ideas of mystery, awe and wonder
- Heaven
- Creation stories

History
- Modern American/Russian History
- Development of space travel
- Men on the Moon
- Astronomy (Gallileo etc.)

P.E.
- Travelling, using different speeds, directions, levels

Outer space
(Places)

Music
- Planet suite
- Compose own sound effects for imaginary planet. Devise notation for them and record

Science
- Astronomy
- Our planet and universe (ATs 15.5,16.4)

Maths
- Calculations using large numbers
- Infinity (AT 2.4)

Descriptions (theme: Literature)

Pupil's book pages	Activities	Understanding and skills	Attainment targets*

26–27
Describing action
	Looking at descriptions of action	Style:
		  Analysing techniques
		  Use of verbs
		  Creating pace
		  Linking action to background
			
			1.4, 2.4
			1.5, 2.5
			2.6
			3.4, 3.5, 3.6, 4/5.5

	Writing about a chase or pursuit		

28–29
Describing people
	Looking at extract and poem	Style:
		  Analysing techniques
		  Economy
		  Selection of ideas
		  Implication
		  Creating an impression
			
			1.4, 2.4
			1.5, 2.5
			1.6, 2.6

	Writing about a character		3.4, 3.5, 3.6, 4/5.5

30–31
Describing places
	Looking at extract	Style
		  Use of adjectives
		  Use of nouns
		  Selection of ideas
		  Creating a mood
		  Nouns that epitomise places
			
			1.4
			1.5
			2.4, 2.6
			
			2.5

	Writing about a place	Description Drafting and redrafting	3.4 3.5, 3.6, 4/5.5

* Key to Attainment Targets
1 Speaking and Listening
2 Reading
3 Writing

The number before the point relates to the Attainment Target in the National Curriculum. The number after refers to the level.

Focus and aims of the unit

This unit focuses on three kinds of description. The first section looks at writing about action and examines how writers achieve a sense of speed and movement. The next section asks the children to look at two very different descriptions of people and demonstrates how an author, by writing about the way a character talks and behaves, can create an impression of that person without actually describing what he or she looks like. Using a single extract, the third section demonstrates how a description of a place can create a sense of atmosphere, and discusses how an author has to select aspects of that place to give an impression of it to the reader.

Pages 26–27 Describing action

Two extracts are used in this section. The first describes a chase across difficult and hostile countryside so that the description of the dangerous terrain, in particular the swollen stream, lends excitement to the passage.

The second builds up the tension slowly and shocks the reader with the suddenness of the two boys' fear, and the terrified attempt of one of them to run away. The fear and sudden terror is given point by the coldness and almost menacing slowness of the boys' pursuers.

Looking at the first passage

Often, to achieve pace, a writer will use several words for the same action. This piece of writing demonstrates this particularly well where Ryan crashes down the ravine to the stream's edge, e.g. 'as he *jumped* down into the ravine, *slipped* on banked snow, *fell*, *rolled* and *bounced* to his feet.'

There are other similar examples in the passage: the description of the stream, the fickle nature of the bridge of branches, the tumble of Sandor into the water. Looking for these main verbs will identify the words that create the action. Ask the children to say what impression of speed and action they create.

Look for the verbs ending in -ing (present participles): 'racing', 'foaming', 'spanning', 'bursting', 'sending', 'leaping', 'crashing', 'pitching', 'tumbling'. What about the two -ing words in the last sentence – 'swirling', and 'spinning'? How is their use slightly different from the other -ing words? (The first examples have the function of verbs in the passage, whereas 'swirling' and 'spinning' are used as adjectives.) You could use this example to discuss with children how the same words can be either verbs, adjectives or nouns depending on how they are used in the sentence.

Looking at the second passage

The power of the writing in this passage hinges on the gradual realisation on the part of the boy that the man is watching their progress down the drive. Here David Line cleverly repeats the word 'winking', first to describe the fairy lights, then repeating it four more times, each time investing it with more significance until the reader understands that it is the source of fear and danger.

The author takes an entire paragraph to describe the man. The detail about the turned-up collar and silk scarf, the fact the man is leaning on the gate, smoking a cigar and smiling, is particularly chilling, as the writing slows and checks itself before the next paragraph.

Ask the children to say how the last paragraph releases the fear and tension. What is the picture of Soldier from the way his fear is described? What is the effect of the words 'squeak', 'gasp', 'scuttled', 'sliding', 'slipping', 'whimpering'? What is the power of the last sentence?

Extension work

Thinking about words – brain-storming
Think of as many verbs as you can that describe movement. Here are some:

ran	scrambled	scuttled
slid	limped	hobbled
jumped	hopped	stepped
leaped	tiptoed	wriggled
squirmed	rolled	tumbled
bounced	slipped	raced

Get the children to use a thesaurus to find groups of words that might be used to describe actions such as:

something falling, an avalanche, a sinking ship, a car going out of control, a cat hunting a mouse and so on.

Look at further examples of writing from children's authors, to look for the way action is described.

Pages 28–29 Describing people

The section on describing people contrasts two very different pieces of writing. The extract from *The Pinballs* by Betsy Byars is a brilliant pen portrait of the girl, Carlie. The questions in the pupil's book ask the children to give their impression of her. You might ask the children to say what they think her physical appearance is. (Emphasise that the cartoons on pages 28–29 are just one person's idea of what Aunt Sue and Carlie look like.) What do they imagine she would wear? Ask them to say what they think of her manners. Why did she resent everyone? Is it likely that she was well-liked and popular? What had made her so tough, rude, selfish and unfriendly?

The poem by Kelly Brown shows how the effectiveness of describing someone or something depends on the images that the writer chooses. Kelly has encapsulated Aunt Sue in very few words, yet we get a very full idea of what she is like.

Writing a description of a person

Suggest that the children make a list of impressions of someone they know well. They could do this by thinking of two or three things about a person's appearance, two or three about mannerisms and ways of behaving and two or three about what the person does.

Pages 30–31 Describing places

Shirley Hughes provides a wonderfully rich description of Uncle Owen Bowen's big, old house beside the river. In the description, we are transported (rather like a film camera might zoom in) from a 'long shot' of the row of houses, in to Owen Bowen's house. The front door opens and we pass through the hall up the stairs to the room on the top floor where the eccentric old man lives.

The description has some sure touches and children will be able to identify those that are particularly effective. How about 'the steely, oily, muddy, tidal, glittering River Thames'? Talk about the choice of adjectives, their imagery and the sounds they make. They give an impression of something both beautiful and ugly.

The author uses a very powerful simile to describe the house: 'like a rotting tooth in a row of gleaming white ones'. Ask the children how well they think this image works. Discuss similes and ask for examples.

The hall is described by way of its smells. It is easy to forget the senses of smell and sound when writing description. Talk about how smells, both pleasant and not so pleasant, are a part of the atmosphere of a place – school, a hospital, the library, a church, mosque or temple and so on.

In the final paragraph, Shirley Hughes chooses particular items to describe. These items reflect Uncle Owen Bowen's character. Would these have been the only items in the room, or has the author been selective? What does this description tell us about Uncle Bowen?

This section could be linked with the unit on Doors and rooms in *Project English*, Book 2.

Using photocopiable sheet G on page 34

Whereas the questions in the pupil's book concentrate on the style of writing, the questions on the sheet ask children to look more closely at the content of the passage to answer the questions.

Extension work

1 Ask the children to think of another room, or the interior of a building, for example a church, temple or mosque, an indoor swimming pool, the school hall, a dentist's or doctor's waiting room, the village hall, the children's room of a pub, a room in their grandparent's house, and so on.

Ask them to write down one or two items that, as they remember the room, give the strongest impression of it, or which stand out most in their memories. Ask them to do the same thing with one or two of the other senses, such as smell or sound. Like this:

Smell   – a damp, wet sort of smell
         – a smell of chlorine
Sounds – shrieks and splashes
         – shrill, echoing sounds
Touch – the feel of the cold shower
         like needles on my skin

How quickly could the rest of the group tell where this was? Talk about the lists and ask for volunteers to read theirs out.

2 Use the five senses to order description of places or events. Like this:

Sight	Smell	Touch	Sound	Taste
The bright glow of coal on the fire. The old man's rocking chair	The pungent smell of pipe tobacco	The rough coat of the dog on the rug	The clink of teacups and the sound of tea being poured	The taste of scones and butter

Links with other areas of the curriculum

A topic web is not appropriate for this unit as description in itself is not a topic but a mode of writing or speaking which may be applied across the curriculum. Here is a summary of the uses of description in other subject areas:

Classifying: placing objects into categories, e.g. saucepans, whisks, spatulas are kitchen utensils; spades, forks, rakes, hammers, saws are tools; spades and forks are gardening tools.

Definitions: saying what an object is, its size, shape, components, consistency and material, its function and use.

Describing principles: stating the principle by which something works or operates, e.g. a skateboard, a nylon-tip pen.

Describing processes: saying how something is done, such as how to mend a puncture, or how a cake is made.

Giving explanations: arranging information in such a way that the reader can easily understand the facts set before her/him, e.g. explaining why a rainbow forms, explaining how a hurricane starts, explaining a chess move.

Making comparisons: looking at the differences and similarities, making analogies and drawing conclusions.

Descriptions both literary and technical may be used in some of the following ways:

History: Description of places and events
            Biographies of historical figures
            Factual recording of data

Science:	Writing reports Defining Describing principles Giving explanations Recording observations	P.E.:	Explaining rules for games Mirroring movement with partner Expressing feeling or mood through movement
Geography:	Describing landscape, terrain etc. Explaining systems (farming, weather etc.) Using keys and legends	Design:	Instructions to work from Giving instructions for an operation (e.g. a model) Plans and diagrams
R.E.:	Recounting stories Describing festivals and celebrations	Art:	Observational drawings Recording colour mixing and matching Discussing and/or explaining photographs Comparing figurative and symbolic art
Maths:	Symmetry (AT 11.5) Explaining how a solution has been arrived at (AT 1.5)		
Music:	Use of terms (pulse, pitch, rhythm) Word pictures of pieces of music Notation Echoing rhythm or tune		

What's on? (theme: Communications)

Pupil's book pages	Activities	Understanding and skills	Attainment targets*
32–33 **What's on?**	Talking about television Conducting a survey	Discussion and opinion Interpreting results Presentation of data	1.4 1.5 1.6
	Thinking about types of programme	Classifying and subclassifying	3.4
		Vocabulary Research Interpreting data Assimilating information	3.5 2.4, 2.5
34–35 **The camera's eye**	Thinking about programme making – camera techniques	Analysis Research Scripting Viewing critically Making judgements	1.4, 2.4, 2.5 1.5 1.6 3.4 3.5
36–37 **Points of view**	Discussing an issue Holding a formal discussion or debate	Analysing arguments Expressing opinions	1.4 1.5
	Writing a letter of complaint or support	Formal letter writing	1.6, 3.4, 3.5

* Key to Attainment Targets
1 Speaking and Listening
2 Reading
3 Writing

The number before the point relates to the Attainment Target in the National Curriculum. The number after refers to the level.

Focus and aims of the unit

The study of television has always been difficult and elusive. Programmes are ephemeral, their appeal is finite and subject to change. It is only recently that the nature of television, its techniques, and its effects and influence have been included in media education in schools.

The aim of this unit is to give children an insight into television as a medium: to categorise and analyse different types of programme, looking, in a simple way, at their purpose and appeal.

The unit attempts to give the children a simple insight into the way that the programme makers use the camera as the viewer's eye. It asks the children to watch critically and to analyse the camera's work.

Finally the children are asked to think about the influence of television and to discuss the effects that it has on all of our lives in forming our attitudes, modifying our behaviour, and informing, educating and entertaining us.

Pages 32–33   What's on?

The children will need help with the brainstorming exercise. They will be familiar with many of the categories, for example, cartoons, quizzes, sport. They may be less sure of the term 'soap opera' and will find it hard to know how to classify programmes like *Blue Peter* and the Saturday morning children's compilation programmes, that include cartoons and quizzes.

The point of the exercise is to give the children a broad understanding of programming, and you need not worry too much if you make arbitrary decisions about how your categories work out. For example, you may feel that there is a category called 'competition programmes' (including items like *Treasure Hunt* and *The Krypton Factor*) where there is a blurred line between quizzes and sport.

Extension work

Make headings of the main categories. Ask children to make collages or displays for each one by cutting up the *TV Times* and *Radio Times*, and other programme guides and magazines. Combine these displays with the children's own writing – such as comment, programme reviews, letters and surveys.

Pages 34–35 The camera's eye

It will be difficult to make the most of this section if you are unable to demonstrate camera shots by watching a video. You may like to prepare for this by recording a suitable extract from a popular programme and watching it with the children with certain aims in view, for example: to time the length of each scene; to count the number of characters involved; to decide which of the characters said most or was most dominant; to decide what emotion was being expressed – anger, tension, humour, sadness, worry, aggression – as the point of the scene; to see whether the scene showed action or dialogue.

From this kind of analysis, you can begin to determine how the camera was used. How did it show emotion on people's faces? Did it focus on certain objects to express some image relevant to the story or mood of the story? What markers did it show to 'clue the viewer in' – such as a dirty, litter-strewn alley or a sink full of dirty plates? Use this analysis to discuss the programme. What did the children like about it? What was particularly effective? Did the programme makers succeed in creating the dramatic effects?

Extension work

Ask the children to prepare a short review of a programme, such as an episode from their favourite soap opera or drama or situation comedy. Don't make this too ambitious. All that should be required is for the children to comment on a programme or – better still – an incident within a programme. Here you are looking for a simple analysis of what was dramatically and visually effective, as well as an affirmation of the enjoyment, humour, excitement etc. that it gave.

Children will not become TV critics overnight, so don't expect a great deal. Their ability to analyse and be critical is undeveloped. However, by praising interesting comments about programmes and by asking questions yourself, you will begin to open the children's eyes to the medium itself and not just the message.

Pages 36–37 Points of view

Ask the children to imagine the scene from the programme *Our School* which involved the two characters Emma and Fran. What do they suppose might have led the two girls to go shoplifting? A worksheet is provided to allow the children to envisage a scenario (see below).

The point of the section is to provide children with an opportunity to think about the influence of television. Do programmes about children being bad or doing wrong make us horrified and uncomfortable, or do we tend to think that children are entitled to behave badly, and that this is the 'stuff of drama'?

It would be interesting to find out whether children see programmes about crime and naughtiness as 'cautionary tales' with a moral to be drawn and a lesson to be learned.

Using photocopiable sheet H on page 35 – 'Our school'

The worksheet shows the characters in an episode of the children's programme 'Our School' (this is not a real programme but a title made up for this section). The children should work in groups and discuss the characters and the incident, its background, causes and outcome.

Using the information box – holding a discussion or debate

If you decide to hold a debate, you must expect to do a good deal of preparation yourself. The formality of debating will be quite new to children, so you will need to help the main speakers to present a cogent, sustained and logical argument.

Links with other areas of the curriculum

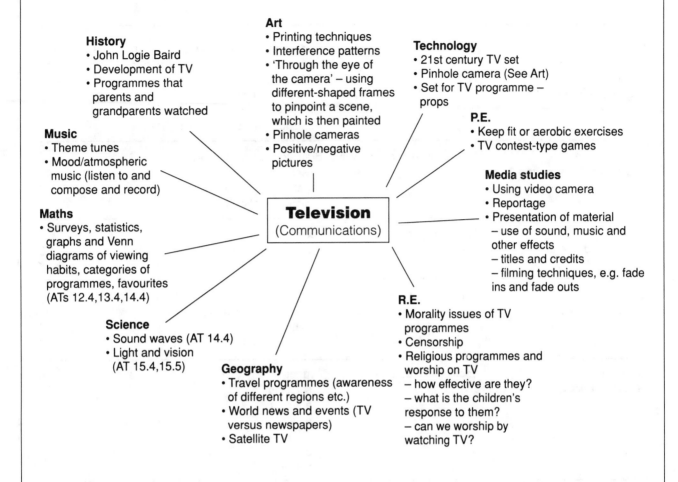

History
- John Logie Baird
- Development of TV
- Programmes that parents and grandparents watched

Art
- Printing techniques
- Interference patterns
- 'Through the eye of the camera' – using different-shaped frames to pinpoint a scene, which is then painted
- Pinhole cameras
- Positive/negative pictures

Technology
- 21st century TV set
- Pinhole camera (See Art)
- Set for TV programme – props

Music
- Theme tunes
- Mood/atmospheric music (listen to and compose and record)

P.E.
- Keep fit or aerobic exercises
- TV contest-type games

Maths
- Surveys, statistics, graphs and Venn diagrams of viewing habits, categories of programmes, favourites (ATs 12.4,13.4,14.4)

Media studies
- Using video camera
- Reportage
- Presentation of material
   – use of sound, music and other effects
   – titles and credits
   – filming techniques, e.g. fade ins and fade outs

Television
(Communications)

Science
- Sound waves (AT 14.4)
- Light and vision (AT 15.4,15.5)

R.E.
- Morality issues of TV programmes
- Censorship
- Religious programmes and worship on TV
   – how effective are they?
   – what is the children's response to them?
   – can we worship by watching TV?

Geography
- Travel programmes (awareness of different regions etc.)
- World news and events (TV versus newspapers)
- Satellite TV

Writers' workshop

Pupil's book pages	Activities	Understanding and Skills	Attainment targets*
38–39 **Organising information 1**	Brainstorming a topic	Brainstorming techniques Thinking of questions Organising information Headings and sub-headings	1.4, 1.5 1.6, 3.4, 3.5
40–41 **Organising information 2**	Making an information web	Brainstorming techniques Research Organising information diagrammatically	2.4, 2.5 2.6
42–43 **Written and spoken** **English**	Reading speech Reading a letter	Looking for differences between speech and writing	1.4, 1.5, 1.6, 2.5, 2.6

44–45
Writing letters 1
	Looking at letters	Register
		Different kinds of letter:
		   personal
		   non-personal (formal)
			3.4, 3.5,
			3.6
			1.4, 1.5
			1.6

46–47
Writing letters 2
	Looking at letters	Format:
		   salutation
		   address
		   ending
		   style
		   content
		Drafting
			2.5, 2.6

* Key to Attainment Targets
1 Speaking and Listening
2 Reading   The number before the point relates to the Attainment Target in the National
3 Writing   Curriculum. The number after refers to the level.

Focus and aims of the unit

The Writers' workshop aims to provide children with approaches to learning about being a writer. It looks at particular kinds of writing and suggests practical ways to help children plan and organise their work. This unit looks at three separate elements: the organisation of information, the differences between written and spoken English, and letter writing.

Pages 38–39 Organising information 1

This section offers children a suggestion for organising and developing ideas generated in a brainstorm session.

Children working individually could try organising the first stages of their work into headings and subheadings. Next, they could research and write up their work under each heading and then finalise the order. For children working in groups, this can provide a way of dividing the work up between the group, so that each individual can take one section to work on.

It could be linked with the sections relating to drafting and planning in the Writers' workshop in Book 1, and also the section on Chapters and paragraphs in the Writers' workshop in Book 3.

The talking and writing section could be used as an example which you work through with the children before they try using the method on one of their current topics.

Pages 40–41   Organising information 2

Making an information web is a variant on the brainstorming technique, whereby the information is recorded in a slightly more organised way. As the information box tells children, each arm of the web takes one idea/feature/aspect related to the main subject. Additional information is added along the same arm. This technique is sometimes known as 'cluster writing'. It is particularly useful for topic planning. It can record, as in the two examples, either what information children already know or what information they require. It is possible to combine these two functions, very usefully, for research purposes. If children first make a web of what they know about the subject in question, they can look at this information and see where there are gaps or areas which they would like to develop. Further arms to the web, or questions on existing arms, can then be added in a different colour pen. From this, children can plan their programme of work.

The talking and writing activities can be done by the children, working alone or in groups, or you can use them as a demonstration to the class or group before they try the webbing idea on a current classroom topic.

Pages 42–43   Written and spoken English

This section looks at the differences between written and spoken English, and could be linked with other work related to register (pp.14–15, 18–19, 36–37).

Children could take each of the comments given on page 42 and find the equivalent written form for it from the letter on page 43. The differences could then be discussed. There may be further examples you could take from the classroom, by tape-recording a discussion of work which is subsequently written up. The differences could be found and talked about.

The information box refers to dialect, and it may be interesting for you to borrow a tape of examples of dialect from the local library for children to listen to. There may also be certain dialect words in common usage in your area, which children could list and talk about. This issue is a sensitive one, and care should be taken that children do not see dialects other than Standard English as inferior or a joke. Just as we wear different clothes for different activities or occasions, so we use Standard English rather than a local dialect for certain purposes.

Pages 44–45   Writing letters 1

The next two sections, on letter writing, look at format, convention and register. This section links with the previous one, contrasting the formal letter with the informal, colloquial style. There may be opportunities for real letter-writing in the work the children are currently engaged in, which could be used with this section. It is better to write a genuine letter to a real person, than a pastiche which will never leave the exercise book. The possibility of receiving a reply is viewed with excitement too, and acts as an incentive to the writer or writers.

Pages 46–47   Writing letters 2

This section focuses rather more on the content of letters. The need for sufficient information and clarity is very important. It is easy to teach the lay-out of letters and overlook the actual content! When children are writing formal letters, it may be helpful for them to plan, or make notes under the headings given at the top of page 46, before they start the actual letter. The points could be numbered, to ensure the sequence is correct and doesn't become fragmented or disjointed.

The information box on page 46 gives children details about how to conclude formal letters.

If children are writing letters to be sent, remember to take photocopies if you want to keep a record of their work!

Nonsense images

Here are two nonsense images from the poem on page 5:

I thought my eyes were big pork-pies,
And my nose was Stilton cheese.

Try writing different nonsense endings to them:

I thought my eyes were _____

My nose was _____

Complete these, as nonsense images:

I floated into _____

A cat with _____

Her hair was _____

It rained _____

Think of two of your own:

_____

_____

_____

_____

_____

 © Roderick Hunt and Tricia Kirkham. *Project English*. Basil Blackwell Ltd.

Wagon train

A wagon train is in trouble. It has lost its way and is now on the edge of a river too wide and deep to cross.

Problem: The pioneers must cross the Sierra Nevada before the winter snows begin in three weeks' time. If they fail they will be snowed in and will die from cold and starvation.

1   If they go back and pick up the Oregon Trail they will waste two weeks. The journey will get them to the Sierra Nevada in three weeks and they may just get across if the snows are late.

2   If they cross the river they will get to the Sierra Nevada mountains in ten days. But how can they cross the river? Each wagon in turn would take two days to prepare and get across. Some might sink or capsize.

3   They could take an unexplored route across the Great Basin. This might get them to the Sierra Nevada in seven days. But there will be boulders, rocks, gulleys and narrow gorges to cross. And there will be no water. Such a journey might take seven days, but it might prove impossible.

There are six wagons in the party, and 21 oxen. There are seven men, eight women and nine children.

Pretend you are the pioneers. Some of you want to go back to the Oregon Trail, some want to risk the unexplored route, and some want to attempt to cross the river. Discuss each option and think of reasons for and against each one. Decide which route might save the party.

© Roderick Hunt and Tricia Kirkham. *Project English*. Basil Blackwell Ltd.

How hurricanes are formed

1   What causes the air over the sea to rise?

_____

_____

2   What is moisture?

_____

3   How are rain clouds formed?

_____

_____

4   Why are huge winds created?

_____

_____

5   How big can the mass of wind and rain become?

_____

_____

6   What causes the mass to spin?

_____

_____

7   How does the spinning make the mass bigger?

_____

_____

8   What is the eye of a hurricane?

_____

   © Roderick Hunt and Tricia Kirkham. *Project English*. Basil Blackwell Ltd.

Before the hurricane

Make this picture into a diagram, using captions and arrows, to point out what precautions to take to make everything as safe as possible for a hurricane.

© Roderick Hunt and Tricia Kirkham. *Project English*. Basil Blackwell Ltd.

Alone on Splatterbang

Write answers to these questions:

What is the starship doing?

_____

_____

What is happening to Mykl as the starship takes off?

_____

_____

What would make you think the starship is quite large?

_____

_____

Why might you think the planet is quite small?

_____

_____

How do you know there is no oxygen on the planet?

_____

_____

Mykl is quite close to the starship when it takes off. What do you think he is trying to do?

_____

_____

How do you know that Mykl doesn't want to be left behind?

_____

_____

Who do you think may be on board the starship?

_____

_____

© Roderick Hunt and Tricia Kirkham. *Project English*. Basil Blackwell Ltd.

Space glossary

atmosphere
(n) the air/gas around a planet

astronaut
(n) a space traveller

blast-off
(n) the moment a rocket or spaceship leaves the ground

boost
(v) to increase or raise, e.g. the power of a motor or jet

crater
(n) a raised up, bowl-shaped hollow or pit, as found on the Moon

cosmic
(adj) to do with the universe

cosmos
(n) the universe

galactic
(adj) to do with a galaxy or galaxies

galaxy
(n) a group of stars in the sky

gravity
(n) the pull of the Earth or a planet; it makes things fall down to the ground

lunar
(adj) belonging to, or to do with, the Moon

module
(n) a separate unit that is part of a bigger construction

meteor
(n) a shooting star

orbit
(n) the regular path of a planet or other body moving round another in space
(v) to go round in an orbit

oxygen
(n) one of the gases in the air – the one we need to breathe

planet
(n) one of the large solid masses, like the Earth, which orbit round the Sun

satellite
(n) 1. a planet or body which goes round a larger one, e.g. the Moon 2. a man-made object that orbits the Earth in space

void
(n) the emptiness that exists beyond the Earth's atmosphere

1 What is the name of the gas we need to breathe? _____

2 What is the name of the air or gas that surrounds a planet? _____

3 Look up the meaning of 'blast-off', then write a definition of 'touch-down'.

_____

_____

4 Where would you find a lunar wind? _____

5 What happens to astronauts where there is no gravity?

_____

Uncle Owen Bowen's house

1 Why didn't Uncle Owen Bowen's neighbours think much of his house?

_____

_____

2 How do you know the house was big and roomy?

_____

_____

3 Owen Bowen was 'disconnected' like the doorbells. What impression of him does this give you?

_____

_____

4 What do you think Owen Bowen does for a living?

_____

_____

5 What might make you think he is quite an old man?

_____

_____

6 Which bit of description of Uncle Owen Bowen, or his house, do you like best?

_____

_____

© Roderick Hunt and Tricia Kirkham. _Project English_. Basil Blackwell Ltd.

Our school

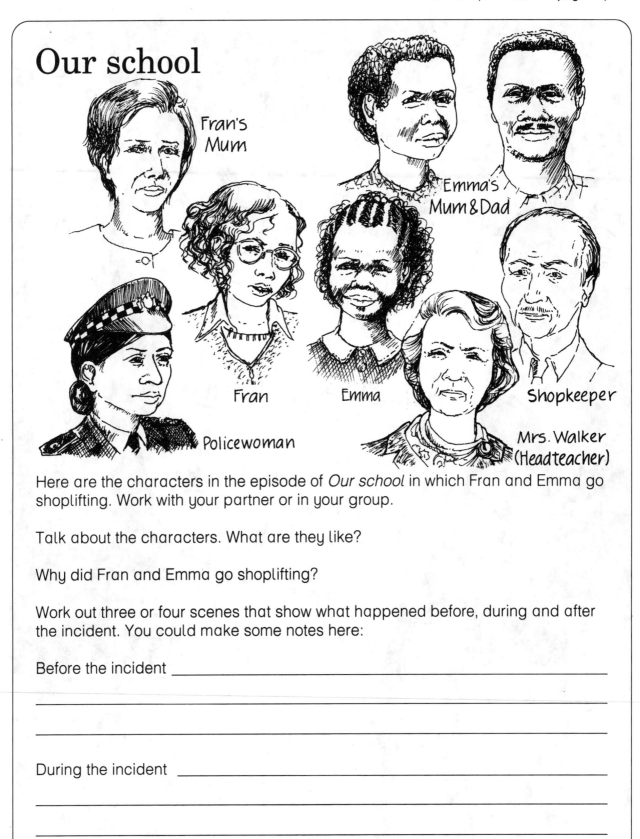

Fran's Mum

Emma's Mum & Dad

Fran

Emma

Shopkeeper

Policewoman

Mrs. Walker (Headteacher)

Here are the characters in the episode of *Our school* in which Fran and Emma go shoplifting. Work with your partner or in your group.

Talk about the characters. What are they like?

Why did Fran and Emma go shoplifting?

Work out three or four scenes that show what happened before, during and after the incident. You could make some notes here:

Before the incident _____

_____

_____

During the incident _____

_____

_____

After the incident _____

_____

_____

You can invent other characters if you like. You don't have to write the episode as a script if you don't want to.

© Roderick Hunt and Tricia Kirkham. *Project English*. Basil Blackwell Ltd.

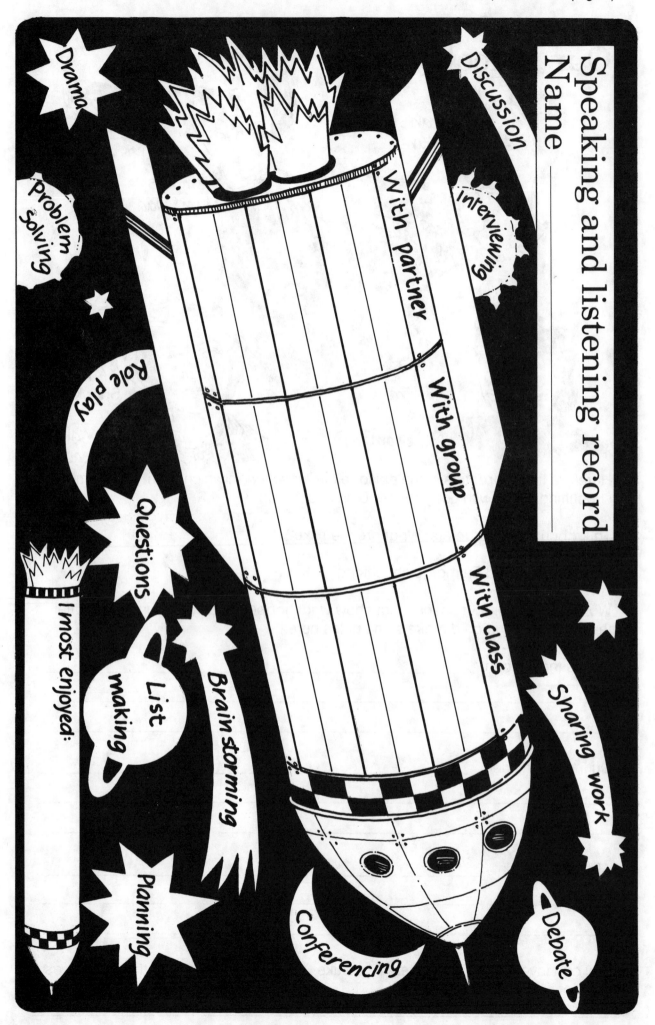

Speaking and listening record
Name

Discussion
Interviewing
With partner
With group
With class
Sharing work
Role play
Drama
Problem solving
Questions
I most enjoyed:
List making
Brainstorming
Planning
Conferencing
Debate

© Roderick Hunt and Tricia Kirkham. *Project English*. Basil Blackwell Ltd.

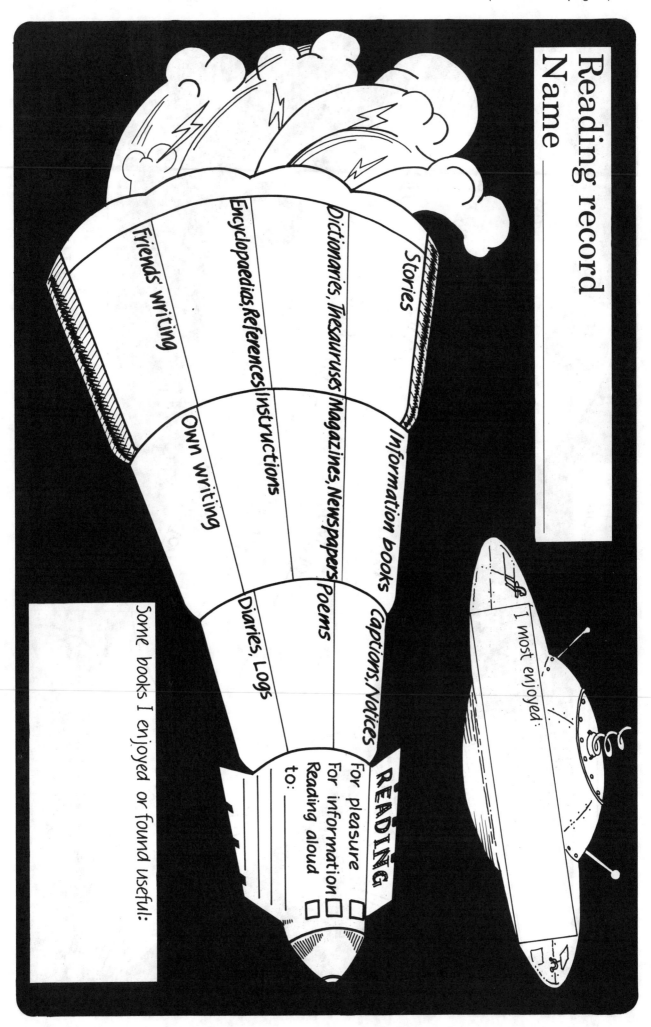

Reading record
Name _____

Stories

Information books

Dictionaries, Thesauruses, Magazines, Newspapers

Encyclopaedias, References, Instructions

friends' writing

Own writing

Diaries, Logs

Poems

Captions, Notices

I most enjoyed:

Some books I enjoyed or found useful:

READING
For pleasure ☐
For information ☐
Reading aloud ☐
to:
_____
_____

© Roderick Hunt and Tricia Kirkham. *Project English*. Basil Blackwell Ltd.

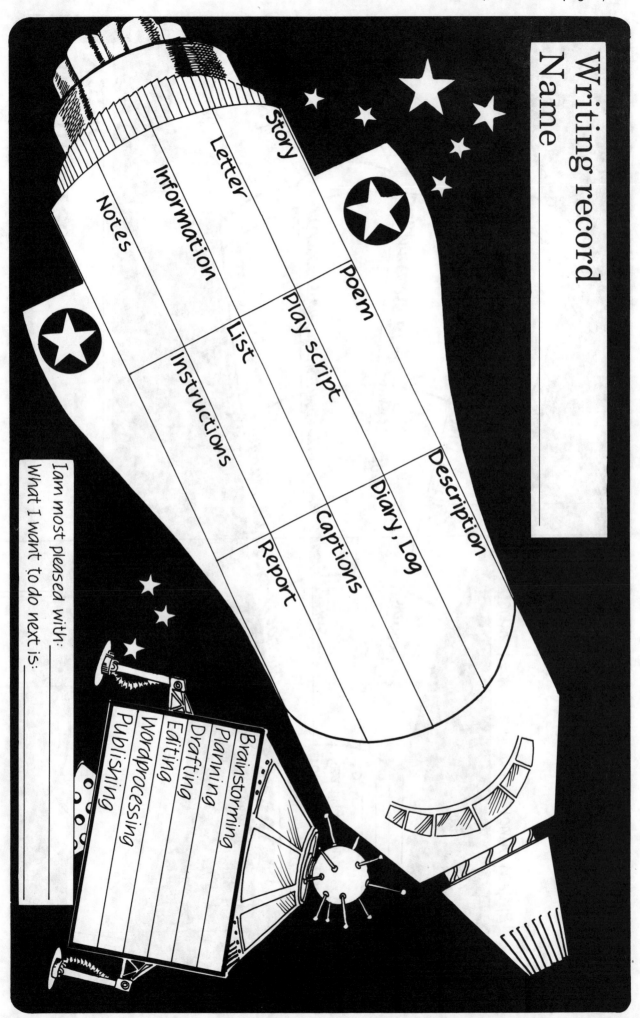

Writing record

Name

Story
Letter
Information
Notes

Poem
Play script
List
Instructions

Description
Diary, Log
Captions
Report

I am most pleased with:

What I want to do next is:

Brainstorming
Planning
Drafting
Editing
Wordprocessing
Publishing

© Roderick Hunt and Tricia Kirkham. *Project English*. Basil Blackwell Ltd.